ELINOR KLIVANS

Cookies

Photography by SIMON WHEELER

THE MASTER CHEFS

TED SMART

ELINOR KLIVANS has won numerous awards for her baking. A native Floridian and graduate of the University of Florida with an honours degree in English and education, she has studied under many noted chefs, both at La Varenne in Paris and at the International Pastry Arts Center under Albert Kumin (formerly pastry chef at the Four Seasons restaurant in New York and at the White House).

Her many roles have included those of cookery teacher, demonstration cook and bakery consultant, and for 12 years she worked as a dessert chef at Peter Ott's restaurant in Camden, Maine. Her articles have been published in several magazines, including *Bon Appétit*, and she has appeared on television and radio shows across the United States.

Elinor's book *Bake and Freeze Desserts*, published in 1994, was nominated for a Julia Child Award for first book. She is currently working on *Bake and Freeze Chocolate Desserts* and lives with her family on the northern coast of Maine.

CONTENTS

Since Eve ate apples,

much depends on dinner.

L O R D   B Y R O N

INTRODUCTION

I was lucky to be born into a cookie-baking family, so I've always known that cookies are a surefire way to build a reputation as a good baker. Even my busiest friends find time to bake cookies: maybe it's the small investment in time, the easily available ingredients, the typically successful results, or the way that cookies fit any occasion.

These recipes mix together quickly, employ simple techniques and yield big batches of cookies. It's worry-free cooking that reminds us of how much fun it is to bake. I've chosen some of my favourite cookies that fit all of these criteria. There are Toasted Almond Crescents for afternoon tea, Oatmeal Raisin Crisps to perk up a weekday lunch and Lace Cookies with Pistachio and White Chocolate to end a dinner party. And the rewards are a delicious-smelling house, a full cookie jar and a good deal of sweet satisfaction.

Elinor Klivans

MOCHA SHORTBREAD FINGERS
dipped in chocolate

200 G/7 OZ PLAIN FLOUR

25 G/1 OZ CORNFLOUR

½ TEASPOON BAKING POWDER

¼ TEASPOON SALT

225 G/8 OZ UNSALTED BUTTER,
SOFTENED

1 TABLESPOON INSTANT COFFEE
GRANULES DISSOLVED IN
2 TEASPOONS WATER

150 G/5 OZ ICING SUGAR

225 G/8 OZ GOOD-QUALITY PLAIN
CHOCOLATE, MELTED (PAGE 29)

MAKES 30–40 COOKIES

Preheat the oven to 150°C/300°F/
Gas Mark 2. Sift the flour,
cornflour, baking powder and salt
together. Set aside.

Using an electric mixer, cream
the butter with the dissolved coffee.
Add the icing sugar and beat until
smooth. Add the flour mixture and
mix until a dough forms.

Transfer the dough to
greaseproof paper and press out to
a 20 x 30 cm/8 x 12 inch
rectangle, about 1 cm/½ inch
thick. Cut into strips about 2 x
6 cm/¾ x 2½ inches. Lift the strips
from the paper and place them
2.5 cm/1 inch apart on two
ungreased baking sheets. Bake for
30 minutes.

Leave to cool on the baking
sheets for 10 minutes, then transfer
to wire racks to cool completely.

Dip the shortbread ends in
melted chocolate and remove
excess chocolate by dragging the
bottoms over the edge of a bowl.
Leave on wire racks until the
chocolate sets.

TOASTED ALMOND CRESCENTS

125 G/4 OZ PLAIN FLOUR
½ TEASPOON SALT
125 G/4 OZ UNSALTED BUTTER,
    SOFTENED
85 G/3 OZ ICING SUGAR, SIFTED
½ TEASPOON VANILLA ESSENCE
½ TEASPOON ALMOND ESSENCE
50 G/2 OZ TOASTED ALMONDS
    (PAGE 29), FINELY CHOPPED

MAKES 24 COOKIES
Preheat the oven to 160°C/325°F/
Gas Mark 3. Sift the flour and salt
together. Set aside.

Using an electric mixer, cream
the butter with 25 g/1 oz of the
icing sugar until smooth. Mix in
the vanilla and almond essence and
the toasted almonds, then add the
flour mixture and mix until a
dough forms.

Taking about 2 teaspoons of
dough at a time, form into 6 cm/
2½ inch long cylinders. Taper the
ends and curve into crescent
shapes. Place the crescents 2.5 cm/
1 inch apart on an ungreased
baking sheet. Bake for about 25
minutes or until the ends and
bottoms of the cookies are golden.

Transfer to a wire rack and
leave to cool for 15 minutes.

Sift the remaining icing sugar
into a bowl. Roll the cookies in
the sugar until they are evenly
coated (you will not use all of the
sugar). Return the cookies to the
wire rack to cool completely.

OATMEAL RAISIN CRISPS

125 G/4 OZ PLAIN FLOUR
½ TEASPOON BAKING POWDER
½ TEASPOON BICARBONATE OF
   SODA
½ TEASPOON SALT
1 TEASPOON GROUND CINNAMON
125 G/4 OZ UNSALTED BUTTER,
   SOFTENED
125 G/4 OZ CASTER SUGAR
125 G/4 OZ LIGHT BROWN SUGAR
1 LARGE EGG
2 TABLESPOONS GOLDEN SYRUP
1 TEASPOON VANILLA ESSENCE
150 G/5 OZ MEDIUM OATMEAL
150 G/5 OZ RAISINS

MAKES 24 COOKIES

Preheat the oven to 180°C/350°F/ Gas Mark 4. Butter two baking sheets. Sift the flour, baking powder, bicarbonate of soda, salt and cinnamon together. Set aside.

Using an electric mixer, cream the butter with the caster sugar and brown sugar until very light and smooth. Beat in the egg, golden syrup and vanilla essence, then the flour mixture. Stir in the oatmeal and raisins.

Drop rounded tablespoons of the mixture, 5 cm/2 inches apart, on the prepared baking sheets. Bake for about 15 minutes or until the cookies are golden brown.

Leave to cool on the baking sheets for 5 minutes, then transfer to wire racks to cool completely.

COCONUT BUTTER BALLS

125 G/4 OZ UNSALTED BUTTER,
   SOFTENED
50 G/2 OZ CASTER SUGAR
1 LARGE EGG, SEPARATED
1 TEASPOON VANILLA ESSENCE
1/4 TEASPOON ALMOND ESSENCE
1 TEASPOON GRATED LEMON ZEST
2 TEASPOONS LEMON JUICE
125 G/4 OZ PLAIN FLOUR
85 G/3 OZ DESICCATED COCONUT
24 GLACÉ CHERRY HALVES

MAKES ABOUT 24 COOKIES
Preheat the oven to 150°C/300°F/
Gas Mark 2. Butter a baking sheet.

Using an electric mixer, cream
the butter with the sugar until very
light and smooth. Add the egg
yolk, vanilla and almond essence,
lemon zest and lemon juice and
beat until smooth. Add the flour
and mix until a dough forms.

Roll a rounded teaspoon of
dough between the palms of your
hands to form a 2.5 cm/1 inch
ball, and repeat until all the dough
is used.

Beat the egg white with a fork
until foamy. Dip the balls of dough
in egg white to coat evenly. Roll
the balls in the coconut and place
4 cm/1½ inches apart on the
baking sheet. Press a cherry half
into the centre of each ball. Bake
for about 35 minutes or until the
coconut is golden brown.

Leave to cool on the baking
sheet for 5 minutes, then transfer
to a wire rack to cool completely.

LACE COOKIES
with pistachio and white chocolate

85 G/3 OZ UNSALTED BUTTER
65 G/2½ OZ CASTER SUGAR
3 TABLESPOONS GOLDEN SYRUP
40 G/1½ OZ PLAIN FLOUR
125 G/4 OZ SHELLED, UNSALTED
    PISTACHIO NUTS, COARSELY
    CHOPPED
¼ TEASPOON GROUND CINNAMON
1 TEASPOON VANILLA ESSENCE
½ TEASPOON ALMOND ESSENCE
1 TABLESPOON VEGETABLE OIL
175 G/6 OZ WHITE CHOCOLATE,
    MELTED (PAGE 29)

MAKES 36 COOKIES

Preheat the oven to 180°C/350°F/ Gas Mark 4. Line three baking sheets with strong foil and butter the foil.

Put the butter, sugar and golden syrup into a saucepan and heat until the butter melts and the sugar dissolves. Bring to the boil, stirring constantly, and boil for 30 seconds. Remove from the heat and stir in the flour, then the chopped pistachio nuts, cinnamon, vanilla and almond essence.

Drop teaspoons of the mixture, 8 cm/3 inches apart, on to the prepared baking sheets. Bake for about 10 minutes or until the cookies are evenly golden (reverse the baking sheets after 5 minutes to ensure even browning).

Leave to cool on the baking sheets for 10 minutes, then lift the cookies from the foil on to wire racks to cool completely.

Stir the oil into the melted chocolate. Drizzle the chocolate over the cookies.

ORANGE CHOCOLATE PINWHEELS

125 G/4 OZ PLAIN FLOUR

¼ TEASPOON BAKING POWDER

⅛ TEASPOON SALT

125 G/4 OZ UNSALTED BUTTER,
    SOFTENED

125 G/4 OZ CASTER SUGAR

1 LARGE EGG, SEPARATED

1 TEASPOON VANILLA ESSENCE

1 TEASPOON GRATED ORANGE ZEST

50 G/2 OZ GOOD-QUALITY PLAIN
    CHOCOLATE, MELTED (PAGE 29)

2 TEASPOONS UNSWEETENED
    COCOA POWDER, SIFTED

MAKES 40 COOKIES

Sift the flour, baking powder and
salt together. Set aside.

Using an electric mixer, cream
the butter and sugar. Mix in the
egg yolk and vanilla. Add the flour
mixture and mix until a dough
forms. Cut the dough in half;
flavour half with the orange zest,
half with the chocolate and cocoa.
Form each piece into a 12 cm/
5 inch disc, wrap and refrigerate
until firm, about 2 hours.

Roll out each piece of dough
on greaseproof paper to form a 12
x 25 cm/5 x 10 inch rectangle.
Beat the egg white until foamy,
then brush over the orange dough.
Press the chocolate dough on top.
Trim the edges, then roll up the
two layers to form a tight cylinder.
Refrigerate until firm.

Preheat the oven to 190°C/
375°F/Gas Mark 5. Butter two
baking sheets.Cut the cylinder into
5 mm/¼ inch rounds and place
2.5 cm/1 inch apart on the baking
sheets. Bake for about 13 minutes
or until the edges are light golden,
then transfer to wire racks to cool.

STRAWBERRY SANDWICH HEARTS

175 G/6 OZ PLAIN FLOUR

175 G/6 OZ COLD, UNSALTED
     BUTTER, CUT INTO SMALL
     PIECES

4–5 TABLESPOONS ICED WATER

1 LARGE EGG WHITE

2 TABLESPOONS CASTER SUGAR

3 TABLESPOONS STRAWBERRY JAM

MAKES 18 HEARTS

Preheat the oven to 200°C/400°F/
Gas Mark 6. Line two baking
sheets with nonstick baking paper.

Using an electric mixer on low
speed, mix the flour and butter
until pea-sized pieces form.
Gradually add the water, until the
dough holds together and comes
away from the sides of the bowl.
Form the dough into two discs,
about 10 cm/4 inches in diameter.
Wrap and refrigerate until firm,
about 15 minutes.

Roll out the dough to about
3 mm/$\frac{1}{8}$ inch thick. Cut out hearts
using a 6 cm/2½ inch heart-shaped
cutter. Press the scraps together, roll
out and cut out further hearts –
you should have 36 hearts. Place
2 cm/¾ inch apart on the baking
sheets. Brush with egg white and
sprinkle with sugar. Bake for about
15 minutes, reversing the sheets
after 6 minutes, until the bottoms
of the cookies are golden. Transfer
to wire racks to cool.

Spread jam on the bottom of
18 cookies and press the remaining
cookies on top, bottom side down.

BUTTERSCOTCH BROWNIES
with marble topping

175 G/6 OZ PLAIN FLOUR
1 TEASPOON BAKING POWDER
¼ TEASPOON SALT
150 G/5 OZ UNSALTED BUTTER,
    SOFTENED
250 G/9 OZ LIGHT BROWN SUGAR
1 TEASPOON VANILLA ESSENCE
2 LARGE EGGS
85 G/3 OZ GOOD-QUALITY PLAIN
    CHOCOLATE, MELTED (PAGE 29)

MAKES 16 BROWNIES

Preheat the oven to 180°C/350°F/ Gas Mark 4. Butter a 22 cm/ 9 inch square cake tin, 5 cm/ 2 inches deep.

Sift the flour, baking powder and salt together. Set aside.

Using an electric mixer, cream the butter with the brown sugar and vanilla essence until smooth. Mix in the eggs, then the flour mixture. Spread the mixture in the prepared tin.

Drizzle the melted chocolate over the top. Run a knife through the chocolate to create a marbled effect. Bake for 30–35 minutes or until a small skewer inserted into the centre comes out clean.

Leave to cool in the tin. Cut into 16 brownies.

LEMON CRUMBLE BARS

225 G/8 OZ PLAIN FLOUR

25 G/1 OZ ICING SUGAR, PLUS
    EXTRA, FOR DUSTING

175 G/6 OZ LIGHT BROWN SUGAR

175 G/6 OZ COLD, UNSALTED
    BUTTER, CUT INTO SMALL
    PIECES

LEMON FILLING

3 LARGE EGGS

200 G/7 OZ CASTER SUGAR

85 ML/3 FL OZ LEMON JUICE

2 TEASPOONS GRATED LEMON ZEST

25 G/1 OZ PLAIN FLOUR

MAKES 20–30 BARS

Preheat the oven to 180°C/350°F/ Gas Mark 4. Butter and flour a 22 cm/9 inch square cake tin, 5 cm/2 inches deep.

Using an electric mixer, mix the flour, icing sugar, brown sugar and butter until pea-sized crumbs form. Press half of the crumbs into the bottom of the prepared tin and bake for 15 minutes.

To make the lemon filling, whisk the eggs, sugar, lemon juice and lemon zest until smooth. Add the flour and whisk again until smooth. Pour the lemon filling over the partly baked crust and bake for 20 minutes.

Sprinkle the reserved crumble mixture over the filling and bake for a further 20 minutes.

Leave to cool in the tin. Dust with icing sugar and cut into 20–30 bars.

GINGER SQUARES
with cream cheese frosting

225 G/8 OZ PLAIN FLOUR

1 TEASPOON BAKING POWDER

½ TEASPOON BICARBONATE OF
SODA

½ TEASPOON SALT

2 TEASPOONS GROUND GINGER

1 TEASPOON GROUND CINNAMON

¼ TEASPOON GROUND CLOVES

125 G/4 OZ UNSALTED BUTTER,
SOFTENED

325 G/12 OZ LIGHT BROWN SUGAR

2 LARGE EGGS

4 TABLESPOONS GOLDEN SYRUP

175 G/6 OZ CHOPPED DATES

CREAM CHEESE FROSTING

175 G/6 OZ SOFT CREAM CHEESE

85 G/3 OZ UNSALTED BUTTER,
SOFTENED

1 TEASPOON VANILLA ESSENCE

325 G/12 OZ ICING SUGAR

2 TABLESPOONS CHOPPED
CRYSTALLIZED GINGER

MAKES 36 SQUARES

Preheat the oven to 180°C/350°F/
Gas Mark 4. Butter a 22 cm/
9 inch square cake tin, 5 cm/
2 inches deep. Sift the flour, baking
powder, bicarbonate of soda, salt,
ginger, cinnamon and cloves
together. Set aside.

Using an electric mixer, cream
the butter with the brown sugar.
Mix in the eggs, golden syrup and
dates, then the flour mixture.
Spread the mixture in the prepared
tin. Bake for about 35 minutes or
until a small skewer inserted into
the centre comes out clean.

Leave to cool in the tin. Cut
into 36 squares.

To make the frosting, beat
together the cream cheese, butter
and vanilla essence until smooth.
Add the icing sugar and beat until
smooth. Put the frosting in a pastry
bag fitted with a star tip. Pipe a
swirl of frosting on each square.
Top the frosting with a piece of
crystallized ginger.

THE BASICS

INGREDIENTS

FLOUR
Whenever flour needs to be sifted, I weigh or measure it first, then sift it together with the other dry ingredients.

BUTTER
I always use butter, rather than margarine, for its incomparable flavour in cookies. I use unsalted butter so that I can control the amount of salt in the mixture; salted butter is often too salty.

EGGS
I use eggs graded 'large' (size 1 or 2). They should be allowed to come to room temperature for about 30 minutes before use.

SUGAR
Most cookies are made with caster sugar, but those with a particularly fine texture, such as shortbread, are made with icing sugar. Light brown sugar contributes its delicious rich flavour to darker cookies and cake squares.

EQUIPMENT

ELECTRIC MIXER
I find an electric mixer invaluable, but it is not essential for any of the recipes in this book. Creaming (page 29) can be done by hand (albeit a strong one), using a wooden spoon. Recipes in which flour and butter are mixed to form pea-sized crumbs, such as the lemon crumble bars, can be made by rubbing lightly with your fingertips.

BAKING TINS

For the best results, use the size described in the recipe. I find a 20–22 cm/ 8–9 inch square tin most useful; the smaller size will produce a denser, moister result.

To prevent scorching, use heavyweight baking equipment. Dark-coloured baking sheets and tins absorb heat more rapidly and baking times may have to be shortened.

TECHNIQUES

CREAMING BUTTER AND SUGAR

This is the process of beating butter and sugar together until the mixture is pale in colour, light in texture, well blended and smooth.

MELTING CHOCOLATE

To help chocolate melt evenly, chop the chocolate roughly into about 1 cm/½ inch pieces. Put the chopped chocolate in a clean, dry double boiler or a bowl placed over a saucepan of hot, not boiling, water. Stir the chocolate often, using a dry spoon, until it is melted and smooth.

Alternatively, chocolate can be melted in a microwave oven. Place the chopped chocolate in a small, clean, dry bowl and heat at 100%. At 30-second intervals, remove the bowl from the oven and gently stir the chocolate with a clean, dry spoon. (Timings vary depending on the quantity of chocolate and the power of the oven.)

TOASTING ALMONDS

Spread the almonds in a single layer on a baking sheet. Bake at 160°C/ 325°F/Gas Mark 3 for about 15 minutes until golden.

BAKING TIMES

Check cookies often towards the end of their baking time. If they are browning unevenly, reverse the baking sheet in the oven about halfway through the baking time.

Cookies are usually done when they reach a certain colour – golden or light brown, as described in the recipe – or when their edges turn light brown. To test brownies or cake squares, insert a cocktail stick, toothpick or small skewer into the centre. As soon as the skewer comes out clean the brownies are ready.

THE MASTER CHEFS

SOUPS
ARABELLA BOXER

MEZE, TAPAS AND ANTIPASTI
AGLAIA KREMEZI

PASTA SAUCES
GORDON RAMSAY

RISOTTO
MICHELE SCICOLONE

SALADS
CLARE CONNERY

MEDITERRANEAN
ANTONY WORRALL THOMPSON

VEGETABLES
PAUL GAYLER

LUNCHES
ALASTAIR LITTLE

COOKING FOR TWO
RICHARD OLNEY

FISH
RICK STEIN

CHICKEN
BRUNO LOUBET

SUPPERS
VALENTINA HARRIS

THE MAIN COURSE
ROGER VERGÉ

ROASTS
JANEEN SARLIN

WILD FOOD
ROWLEY LEIGH

PACIFIC
JILL DUPLEIX

CURRIES
PAT CHAPMAN

HOT AND SPICY
PAUL AND JEANNE RANKIN

THAI
JACKI PASSMORE

CHINESE
YAN-KIT SO

VEGETARIAN
KAREN LEE

DESSERTS
MICHEL ROUX

CAKES
CAROLE WALTER

COOKIES
ELINOR KLIVANS

THE MASTER CHEFS

This edition produced for The Book People Ltd,

Hall Wood Avenue, Haydock, St Helens WAII 9UL

Text © copyright 1996 Elinor Klivans

Photographs © copyright 1996 Simon Wheeler

First published in 1996 by

WEIDENFELD & NICOLSON

THE ORION PUBLISHING GROUP

ORION HOUSE

5 UPPER ST MARTIN'S LANE

LONDON WC2H 9EA

British Library Cataloguing-in-Publication data
A catalogue record for this book is available
from the British Library.

ISBN 0 297 83649 8

DESIGNED BY THE SENATE

EDITOR MAGGIE RAMSAY

FOOD STYLIST JOY DAVIES